VITAL INGREDIENTS

GET INTO THE CREATIVE INDUSTRY EASILY
MAKING COOL CASH FULL TIME OR PART TIME
PLUS UNSEEN BUSINESS ANGLES -IN THE ARTS,
FILM, MUSIC AND MEDIA.

VITAL INGREDIENTS IN THE ARTS OF CREATIVE
STORYTELLING, SCREENPLAY, AUTHORING, FILM
PRODUCING, PLUS BUSINESS ANGLES AND JOBS IN
NOLLYWOOD, THE CREATIVE & ENTERTAINMENT
INDUSTRY IN GENERAL.'

A QUEST TO CREATE JOBS, PROMOTE CREATIVITY,
AND PROVIDE FOR THE IMPOVERISHED; ALL IN A
BID TO BETTER THE LIVES OF INDUSTRY PLAYERS.

Written by:
Lucky Odili aka Luciano
Screen play writer, Film producer

(Member SWGN screen writers guild of Nigeria, Nigeria
film producers forum)

Edited by:
Tary West
Screen play writer, film producer and film director.
Secretary general SWGN (screen writers guild of
Nigeria)

1

TABLE OF CONTENT

SESSION B: FILM PRODUCTION

What is Film Production
Who is a Film Producer
How to become a Film Producer
Film Proposal & Budget
How to become a successful Producer
How to make your film attractive
Things to avoid while producing
Time factor
How to start film producing on Part-Time Basis
How to start producing your works on Partnership Basis
How to start small and grow big
How to start big and maintain it
How to locate people to work with
How to get Investors for the business

FILM CREW

TECHNICAL
Director
Director of Photograph (Cinematographer)
Production Designer
Camera Operator
Arts Director
Special Effects Supervisor
Set Designer
Continuity Supervisor
Gaffer
Sound Mixer
Boom Operator
Utility Sound Technician
Key Grip

Crane Operator
Camera Car Driver
Camera Assistant

NONTECHNICAL
Executive Producer
Producer
Line Producer
Casting Director
Casting Associate/Team
Makeup Artist
Costume Designer
Property Master
Location Manager
Still Photographer
Production Assistant
Transport Captain
Transport Managers
Welfare Officer
Set Medic

POST PRODUCTION
What is Post Production

CREW
Editor
Assistant Editor
Colorists
VFX Supervisor
Roto/Paint Artist
Matte Painter
Compositor

Sound Designer
Dialogue Editor
Re-Recording Mixer
Music Supervisor
Sound Editor
Foley Artist

OTHERS WHO PARTICIPATE IN EDITING
Director
Producer
Special Effects Supervisor
Continuity Supervisor
Production Assistant

SOUNDTRACK
What is Soundtrack

CREW
Music Supervisor
Audio Producer
Audio Engineer
Composer
Artiste(s)

SESSION C: NOVEL
How to become a Novelist
How to create story for a Novel
Rules to adhere to when creating a story
How to prepare
Story Title: Deeply In Love
Developing Story into Novel (Summary)
Notes
Becoming a successful Novelist

INTRODUCTION

Vital Ingredients in the arts of creative storytelling, screenplay, authoring, film producing, plus business angles and jobs in Nollywood, the Creative & Entertainment Industry in general.'

Basically, it is a Four-In-One motivational book, designed mainly to create jobs. It is informative, educative and inspiring; written passionately, to spur intending screenwriters, film producers, novelist, and those job seeking in the creative and entertainment industry, Nollywood in particular, either on a part time or full time basis.

This is an expose on the Ingredients needed to get into these arts, and be knowledgeable on how best to mix them (ingredients) in order to prepare a "sumptuous meal." Also in the offering are many unseen business angles, that intending, passionate practitioners can explore, to create jobs for themselves and others; making good money in the process and becoming a success.

To get jobs these days, from government offices/agencies and companies have become increasingly difficult. No doubt, this manual will serve as succour to many that are under the shackles of unemployment, i.e those seeking ways to multiply their streams of income. The Industry has many avenues through which any interested individual can get jobs and better their lives.

The jobs listed in this manual, require a great dose of burning desire from intending practitioners, coupled with devotion and an unquenchable desire to excel; with these qualities, and the information elaborated upon in this manual. The sky will be a starting point.

This manual shall also serve as a source for quality information for Practitioners, as it contains some solutions to problems most face. E.g. Those who have lost intellectual properties to callous individuals, because they the Originators (Creators/Writers) are unable to protect their works. It will also serve as a Guide for those who are not privileged to connect with personalities likely to invest in projects or counsel on how best to involve investors.

There is a connecting link between the arts of screenwriting and film production. Intending practitioners (writers) are greatly encouraged to put into practice, the information in this manual so that they can on their own, produce their works.

This is designed to create jobs, promote creativity, and provide for the impoverished; all in a bid to better the lives of industry players.

DEDICATION

I dedicate this to all the teeming youths that are under the shackles of unemployment, under employment as well as those that are not particularly youths but have a burning desire to excel. This work will serve as a succour to them.

INSPIRATION

I'm inspired to write this manual as a way to contribute to the economic development of the people and the country.

ACKNOWLEDGEMENT

I want to sincerely use this medium to acknowledge some persons that helped shaped my path in the creative industry.

Mr Adim Williams, screen play writer per excellence, film producer of note and able film director as we usually call him.

Tary West, Secretary general of the screen writers guild of Nigeria SWGN, she is also a film producer and director and a business woman.

Mr. Precious Enebuse, the publisher of grassroot trumpet newspaper, he is also a business man.

SESSION A: CREATIVITY
SCREENWRITING

HOW TO CREATE YOUR STORY / THE ART OF SCREENPLAY WRITING

Right from time in the business of film making creative writing has remain the most essential ingredient in the business , without a story there will be no screenplay and without a screenplay there will be no film.

Every film you watch, started first as a story that someone created or someone saw something happen and built a story from it. No matter how bad a film is you will still notice that there is a message in it. Creative story writing is an art of writing a story from a deep feeling about something you really have a strong thought on any subject. In the same vein writing a screenplay is also base on the same kind of feeling you have while writing a story. However story writing is like the normal essay you write or normal letter writing. In story writing for film, you have to be creative, your thinking while writing a story for film may be absurd, it may be stupid, it may be good, it may be bad, it all depends on your mood, or the story you want to tell. Story writing for film is often use by the writer as a catalyst for change; you must as a matter of principle make your story to be one that will affect people positively even if it means that sometimes you have to do so indirectly i.e. in writing your story, you can create your characters as being wicked from the beginning of the story but in the end he/she must pay for being wicked or you could as well transform a wicked character from the beginning of the story to a good character towards the end after he/she must have paid for the wicked acts. You are at liberty to combine two different stories in one work.

In screenplay writing, you breakdown the story and characters into different scenes in your script. It is when writing the screenplay of your story that you will have to be more creative. It is not necessary that you must start your screenplay the way you started your story, sometimes you may have to pick up the screen playing from the middle or the end of your story and start off your screenplay; but you must remain on the story you are telling, and the message you want to pass across. Screenplay writing can take days for you to start off, in preparing to write a screenplay of your story, you first of all think about the way and manner you want your characters to unfold, in a way that people must learn something from your message. You must have it at the back of your mind that in screenplay writing, your characters must transform too just as stated in story writing. In screenplay writing, you will definitely create many more characters, unlike story writing, screenplay writing is wider; there are many steps to be adhered to when writing a screenplay.(see inside)

The key point in screenplay writing is your ability to create situations (suspense) using your characters, and as well finding solutions to the situations (suspense) you have created, this way you will be creating a lot of actions, passing of information and educating people too. In screenplay writing, you can start off your story by being subtle i.e. not letting the cat out of the bag, gradually as you build your screenplay you can begin to

14

let your thoughts out using your characters, by this process, you build suspense; suspense is very vital because it makes your screenplay interesting.

HOW TO CREATE YOUR STORY/ART OF SCREENPLAY

Story can be created from an interest point of view, or from a horrified point of view or maybe from an emotional view angle, comical point of view, religious point of view, cultural point of view, or psychological point of view etc. Including a story too from another party's angle i.e. a story someone else tells you (tell the person about your intention first, you can reach an agreement with the person). The act of creating story is blossomed by your concentrated thinking on a subject matter you feel very passionate about.

You can create your story from anything or any word that attracts you, someone may say something that is interesting to your hearing, from such statement, you can create a story e.g. "they are deeply in love", the term deeply in love to me sounds very interesting, as a creative writer, I can begin to imagine immediately how two people can be deeply in love, you can further imagine them having problems and over coming the problems usually in creating your own story, You are at liberty to choose from what angle to create your story. Stories must be believable I.e. your story must be seen to be capable of happening to anybody either dead or alive. Your story must have a title.

Stories are built around believable characters as stated above, most Nigerian stories are built around 2 or 3 characters, although, it is not mandatory that your story must be built around 2 or 3 characters it could be more or less. However from experience stories built around 2 characters usually gives a writer, the possibility to easily play out his thought through his story, and also allows him to create other characters that will either serve as support characters and minor characters. The 2 characters (or more as the case maybe) that a writer builds his story around are called major or lead characters. The lead characters are the artistes that are telling the story of the writer, the writer uses them to describe his story, in the manner that he (the writer) wants it. Your two or more lead characters can as well oppose them selves depending on the story. The support characters (at times they could be 2 or 3 or more depending on how the writer wants to tell his story). The support characters are the ones that support the lead characters to tell the story of the writer. Sometimes, the writer uses the support characters to antagonize the lead characters, while on the other hand, the writer can as well use the support character as backups to the lead characters to tell his story. It all depends on the way the writer sees his story and the plot of the story unfolding the way the writer wants it. The minor characters are the artistes (characters) that the writer uses to further enhance the telling of his story. The writer in most cases, uses the minor characters to serve both the lead and support characters in his story. In some cases, the writer may use a minor character to play a vital role in telling his story; while most part of the story, will have the lead characters appearing and reappearing either as antagonist or protagonist; atimes, your character may be passive but yet you can still use him/her to play a vital role in your story, by eyes contact, leg movement, finger signs etc.

RULES TO ADHERE TO WHEN SCREENPLAYING

Scenes break down

1.   A screen play broken down into scenes ensures orderliness; it enables the viewers to see your story as it unfolds. it makes it easier for the artistes to understand the character he / she is to play. It ensures that the viewers understand the characters as presented by the writer. The script written out in scenes sequence, make the logistics involve in production to be easily set out. i.e. props, locations, costume, make up (although there are people in charge of providing these in the course of shooting the work into film). You must number your script and indicate your scenes.

SETTINGS: A screen played script must indicate the settings; depending on your story, your settings could be rich or poor or average settings. You may combine two settings or three settings depending on the way you want to tell your story.

OUTSIDE OR INSIDE. A script writer is expected to indicate in his script in a manner with which he sees his story unfolding. i.e. exterior. EXT for short. Exterior stands for shot taken outside an area e.g. front of a house is a good example of outside scene; while on the other hand there is the inside scene which is also known as interior scene INT for short stands for shot taken inside e.g. inside a room is a good example of interior scene. There is no special principle here, you just decide where you want your characters to play out your story depending on your message.

LOCATION:

A script writer must indicate in his shooting script where a shot is to be taken. A sitting room, a bed room, a kitchen, a bathroom, etc. these are examples of interior scenes, in the same vein a shot can be taken in a bush, a road, front of a supermarket, at the top of a roof etc. these are examples of exterior scenes. These are locations that must be indicated in a script by a script writer, just as stated above there is no specific rule to this , you just go ahead and decide how you want it depending on your message and mood.

THE TIME OF THE DAY: in writing your script, you must indicate the time of the day the shot is to be taken e.g. morning, afternoon, evening, night, mid night, in some cases the exact time may be indicated e.g. 9.00am. 13.00hrs, 18.00hrs, 22.000hrs, 0230hrs. It depends on how the writer sees his story unfolding. The names of your characters are very essential in writing your script; you must name your characters with names that are known.

CHARACTER DESCRIPTION: sometimes you may need to describe your Characters (it is important) e.g. age, height, size etc.(thickly bearded, nice hair)(a native doctor most likely to have thick bears). Your story determines these.

DIALOGUE: This is also known as the lines. It is mainly about the words that the artistes will communicate to each other in the course of acting out the story. Dialogues must be in line with the way you want your story to unfold. Dialogue helps a writer to build his/her character(s) as he wishes and a writer can through dialogue transform his character(s), either from good to evil or the other way round too. Your line of story will determine the kind of dialogue you use e.g. if you want to tell someone about how your girlfriend disappointed you, you will not be happy to tell the story. (in telling the story, see yourself and girlfriend as lead characters. After sometime in your narration, your girlfriend mood will change and she will start to oppose you automatically her dialogues change) In order to create suspense as a creative writer, you can start by narrating how both of you started on a good note; in order to elaborate your story, you can picture yourself having two friends,(support characters) look at one of them as someone sympathetic with you while you can picture your second friend as someone mocking you because of the situation you find yourself, you can as well introduce others into your narration either as opposers or supporters to your plight(minor characters). As a creative writer, you should be able to know the kind of dialogues that the various characters will use when writing. Definitely a supporter will always use mild language, while an opposer will use harsh language i.e. if you want to write a story with a good ending, you may decide to start off first making your characters to go through some agony (so as to create suspense) or it can as well be the other way round, depending on the story you want to tell and the message you want to pass across and the lesson you want people to learn from it. It is through dialogue that you entertain, inform and educate people via your script.

MECHANICAL ACCURACY

Your mechanical accuracy is very vital when screen playing. It plays important role in instructing artistes on how to interpret your characters better i.e. full stop, commas, exclamations etc.

INSTRUCTION: is a written down word in the body of a script by the writer which directs the artistes on what to do in the course of acting out his/her role in the script e.g. sit down, stand up, lying on the bed, angrily etc. your story and dialogues you will create for characters will serve as yardsticks for the instructions you will write down in your script.

FADE: Fade is the indicator that you are through with dialogues and situations of a scene. You should try as much as you can to pass a message through the dialogue you create for your characters in each scene.

THE STORY I CREATED

MY STORY TITTLED-DEEPLY IN LOVE (SUMMARY) (AN AD-LIB)

JAMES and JANET attended the same university, while they were in the university they were very serious students. Consequently, they did not think of any thing romance, however seven years after of their studies, they met in Lagos. Before long they started exchanging visits. Expectedly they fell so deeply in love; but there was a problem they had to surmount; James's parents were wealthy while Janet was from a poor home as a result they vehemently opposed the relationship; but James was not going to heed to their objections, the matter became so bad that James had to annoyingly leave his father's house. Fortunately for both lovers, James had an aunt who was older than his father, she came around one day to discover that James had left the house on the account of him loving a low class lady; it was she who made James's mother to realize too that she was from a poor home yet her brother got married to her and no body opposed them so why were they a stumbling block to James and Janet.

The Aunty had to comb virtually every part of Lagos before eventually getting James. James father finance their colorful wedding.

(This is a summary of the story I wrote impromptu) if I am to develop this story for sell, I will add other characters e.g I will introduce how James and Janet fell in love with other persons against their wishes, I will narrate fully how they started with them and how they fought hard to keep them (I mean their forced lovers)

HOW TO SCREEN PLAY THIS STORY ABOVE (MY PATTERN)

SCENE 1-EXT-DAY

James is driving a jeep along a quiet road, suddenly he notice a lady, he looks closely at her, she looks like Janet her former schoolmate, he parks and comes down and walk to her.

James. Excuse me are you not Janet!!!?

Janet. Yes. You are James !!! THEY HUG PASSIONATELY

James. What a surprise, I was just talking about you and Mabel the other day.

Janet. Wow James you are not looking bad at all!!!

James. Thank you!!! you still have your exquisite looks!!!

Janet. Thank you too. Is that your car?

James. Yes my father bought it for me as a special gift after my graduation!!!

Janet. It is beautiful!!!

James. Thank you. So how is life with you?

Janet. BECOMES SOBER. James, it has not been easy, in fact I am just going to get money from a relation for my siblings to use to feed!!!

James. CONCERN ON HIS FACE. Don't worry things will be okay if you believe in God; mean while come let me give you some money. THEY BOTH WALK TO THE CAR, JAMES OPENS THE DOOR AND BRING OUT SOME MONEY AND GIVE TO HER, SHE IS VERY HAPPY AS SHE RECEIVE THE MONEY.

James. Come in let me take you to where you are going!!!

Janet. What about the place you are going?

James. I am not going to anywhere particularly; I am just driving around the area. THEY BOTH ENTER INTO THE CAR.

FADE

SCENE 2 – INT – DAY

JAMES AND HIS MOTHER ARE SITTING INSIDE THEIR BEAUTIFUL AND EXPENSIVELY FURNISHED SITTING ROOM.

James. HAPPY. Mum yesterday I met my former schoolmate after 7 years of our graduation!!!

Mother. You sound so happy talking about this your schoolmate, who is the person?

James. Her name is Janet, Mum you need to see her, she is so beautiful!!!

Mother. Is her parents known within the corridors of power!!!?

James. BECOMES SAD. Mum why are you asking if her parents are known within the corridors of power!!!?

Mother. You are my son; I can see you are falling in love with her, or may be you are actually in love with her!!!?

James. SOBERLY. Actually Mum, I want to ask her for a solid relationship!!!

Mother. I thought as much; as the son of the most powerful minister in the country you need someone who is from a very solid background to fall in love with!!!

James. NOT HAPPY. But mother is it compulsory that she must come from such background!!!?

Mother. SERIOUS. Very compulsory my dear she must be from such background or something very similar to that!!!

James. Mum just wait to see her first, before you talk of background; I believe when you see her, you will like her!!!.

FADE

SCENE 3-INT-DAY

JANET HAS COME TO VISIT JAMES, THEY ARE SITTING INSIDE JAMES'S FAMILY SITTING ROOM ALSO SITTING ARE JAMES'S PARENTS.

James. VERY HAPPY. Mum and Daddy this is Janet, the lady I told you we attended the same university!!!

Mother. VERY HAPPY TOO PRETENTIOUSLY. Wow!!! What a beautiful lady, Janet you are welcome, James has made so much noise about you!!!

Father. HAPPY TOO. Quite deservedly, James is so proud talking about you. You are very much welcome !!!. please feel comfortable!!!

Janet. VERY SHYLY. Thank you very much sir, thank you very much ma!!!

James. Janet pleases excuse me let me get you something to drink. JAMES WALKS OUT OF THE SITTING ROOM..

Mother . SMILING LIGHTLY. So my daughter what is your father's name?

Janet. Dickson, Dickson Okolo

Father. SURPRISE. Dickson Okolo!!!? That name does not ring a bell

Mother. I have never heard that name before!!!

Father. My dear, so where did your father work, or is he still working!!!?

Janet. LOOKING EMBARRASS. Actually, my father worked with the old public works department as a gateman, he is retired now!!!

Mother. VERY SHOCKED. What!!!? And you want to go out with my son!!!?

Father. SHAKING HIS HEAD DEJECTEDLY. This is unbelievable!!! How on earth can James do this!!!?

Janet. FEELING SO EMBARRASS, JAMES ENTERS HOLDING A CAN OF JUICE, DROPS IT ON A SMALL TABLE HE NOTICE THE FROWN ON JANET'S FACE.

James. SURPRISE. Janet what is the matter!!!? SHE IS MUTE, JAMES GLANCE AT HIS PARENTS

Father. James what do you want from this girl!!!?

James. VERY SURPRISE. Dad what sort of question is that!!!?

Mother. Didn't I ask you the same question the other day!!!?

Janet. STANDS UP HEAD BOW AND WALK OUT

James. SAD. What is the meaning of this dad and mum, it is not fair why have you embarrassed my guest!!!?

Father. James get it right, if she is just your guest, no problem, however if you want to go out with her, she is not the type!!!

James. Dad this is just not fair. HE RUSH OUT, BUT JANET IS GONE AWAY, HE IS NOT HAPPY.

FADE.

SCENE 4 –EXT-DAY

JAMES AND HIS FATHER ARE SITTING AT AN EXQUISITE ANGLE IN FRONT OF THEIR BEAUTIFUL AND MIGHTY MANSION

Father. My son don't you know such girl is not good for you!!!?

James. SAD LOOKING. But dad what is wrong with Janet!!!? Isn't she beautiful enough to be my girlfriend!!!?

Father. Beautiful yes; but my son if you want girls that are even more beautiful than Janet and from rich homes too, I can introduce some of them to you to choose from.

James. No dad, you can't introduce anybody to me, I have the right to choose for myself!.

Father. You are quite right there my son, but if you want to choose, choose from the right source, not somebody from the slum, o come on James give me a break; where is your thinking cap!!?

James. ANNOYINGLY STAND UP. Dad, it is Janet I want to be my girlfriend!

Father. ANGRILY. Then you must be joking, James you are joking! I mean how can you stand here and tell me you want to go out with a nobody; have you forgotten my status in the society!!!?

James. ANGRILY WALK AWAY.

Father. James come back here, I say come back here!!.

FADE.

SCENE 5 NIGHT-EXT

JAMES IS INSIDE HIS CAR LOOKING VERY ANNOYED, HE BLARE HIS HORN AND THE GATEMAN OPENS, HE DRIVE OFF.

Gateman. Oga James where you dey go this night!!!? HE DRIVES OFF

SCENE 6- EXT- DAY

JAMES IS INSIDE HIS CAR, MAKING AN ENQUIRY FROM TWO YOUNG BOYS ABOUT JANET, AFTER A WHILE, HE GETS DOWN FROM THE CAR, AND ENTERS INTO A HOUSE, IT IS A FACE ME I FACE YOU HOUSE, HE KNOCKS ON A DOOR, JANET COMES OUT SEE HIM AND FROWNS.

Janet. James who are you looking for here!!!?

James. VERY SOBER. Janet, I came to apologize to you, I understand how you feel after my parents behaved rudely to you!!!

Janet. James you don't have to apologize they are your parents, if they feel I am not good enough for you, I don't think there is anything you can do about that!!!

James. PASSIONATELY HOLD HER. Janet that is not true; fine they are my parents, but they can't decide for me who to go out with!!!

Janet. LOOKING DEEP INTO HIS EYES. SO James what do you intend to do now that your parents don't want me?!!!

James. STILL HOLDING HER. I believe if we prove to them that we are deeply in love, they will have no option than to support us!!!

Janet. Honestly, I think that will be difficult to achieve. I am sorry to say that your parents are arrogant!!!

James. I know, but if we stick to our love they will have a change of attitude towards you!!!

Janet. James your parents don't want you to go out with someone like me, so leave it that way!!!

James. No Janet, I can't leave it that way, and for your information I have move out of the house.

Janet. Why!!? It is not necessary!!!

James. It is necessary; I am presently staying with a friend!!!

FADE

SCENE 7-INT-DAY

JAMES FATHER'S ELDER SISTER (AUNTY DAYO) ALONG WITH JAMES'S FATHER ARE SITTING INSIDE THEIR (JAMES FATHER'S) EXQUISITE SITTING ROOM.

Elder sister. LOOKING SURPRISE. I am just wondering, where is James? I have been in this house for 10minutes and have not seen him around, that is unusual!!

James's father. You won't believe it, for the past 3days we have been looking for him!!!

Sister. SHOCKED. Where has he gone to, didn't he tell anybody!!!?

Father. He did not mention anything to anybody about his where about!!!

Sister. Did he quarrel with anybody!!?

Father. No!!! actually, he brought one girl from a poor home and said he wanted to fall in love with her, but we advised him against such action, considering her poor status!!!

Sister. ANGRY. Absolute rubbish, Charles this is absolute rubbish, why would you and your wife dissuade a young man from following his heart desire!!?

Father. But aunty, the girl is from a poor home James cannot go out with just a low status girl!

Sister. STILL ANGRY. Charles, how come you have forgotten so soon, that when you married James's mother, she was from a very poor home; you helped her to become who she is today, now she wants to send away a girl from a poor home, that is absolute rubbish

FADE

SCENE8-EXT-DAY

JAMES FATHER'S SISTER IS COMING DOWN FROM HER CAR, SHE IS MAKING A CALL; JAMES-------------- I have been trying to get you on line -------------------- why have you refused to pick your parents call!!?------------------- Okay James my darling I understand your part -------------- okay don't worry I have trashed the issue out with them, so you can return home. SHE HANGS UP SMILLING AS SHE WALKS INTO HER EXQUISITE COMPOUND.

FADE

SCENE 9-INT-DAY

JAMES, HIS PARENTS ALONG WITH JANET AND HIS FATHER'S ELDER SISTER (AUNTY DAYO) ARE SITTING INSIDE THEIR EXQUISITE AND BEAUTIFUL SITTING ROOM.

Mother. VERY SOBERLY. Janet, I want to personally apologize to you for all the heart aches I have caused you; I must confess, I was the one who encouraged my husband not to welcome you!!!

Janet. VERY SHYLY. Thank you ma for accepting me!!!

Father. Personally, I will apologize to both of you James and Janet, I am really sorry for everything.

Aunty Dayo. Well it is alright. But Chares, I am of the opinion that you have to promise them something to make them happy!!

Father. Okay, that is no problem. I am going to give Janet a job; and anytime that they are ready to get married, I will personally sponsor it!!!

END OF SCREEN PLAY FADE

Did you notice the lead characters in the story? James and Janet

Did you notice the support characters? James parents and Aunty Dayo

Did you notice the minor characters? The gateman and the boys

Did you notice how dialogues led to instructions change the characters moods in scenes?

Did you notice the props e.g. cars, can juice, handset, some money?

NOTES: This is just a format of how a script should look like although, you are at liberty to use brackets and small letters (open and close a bracket) to indicate your instructions.

1. A normal script for film production contains up to 60 scenes or more depending on how you feel about your story.

2. Once you master the art of screen play writing, you don't need to write down your story anywhere; you can just go ahead and start off with your screenplay writing. The biggest secret of creative writing is to continually show passion for it.

3. If you are finding it difficult to build up your story, (creating suspense) you can pick up any current issue going on in the society to do so, you can do it comically

or emotionally etc. point of view, you can do so with your main characters or other characters but don't do so for too long. You must maintain your line of thought (the story).

If I am to write this story (the screenplay in full), I will use scenes I have created here as the last part of the screenplay. I will first start by creating suspense i.e. I will imagine Janet being in love with another young good looking man from a poor home but has a steady off and on job and her parents are strongly in support of the relationship. While on the other hand, I will imagine James being in love with another beautiful lady through his mum's arrangement, whilst James was not seriously in love with her, his mother kept assuring the lady that he would marry her, the lady was happy and was making noise about town that she was going to marry James, I will create a lot of situations around these characters up till about 25 to 30 scenes before I will introduce where James and Janet will meet; with the two other characters fighting to keep their relationships. These situations will involve a lot of actions. I will move my characters around to e.g offices, hotels, houses. e.tc In creating your suspense, it must not be predictable; you must keep your viewers in suspense.

HOW TO PREPARE YOUR STORY

As stated earlier, you pick up any topic you feel very passionate about. The topic must be one that people must learn from; within 3days, you can start imagining about 2 or 3 characters that you use to narrate your story.

Thereafter within another 3days, you can gradually start developing your characters the way you want them base on your story, creating dialogues for each of your characters, naturally you will find out that in the course of developing your characters through dialogues, you will see the need to be adding additional characters other than the 2 or 3 you use in your story narration. In a single day, you can create 10 scenes or more; consequently within 10 days you can create 100 scenes of your story i.e. screenplay maybe less, so far you tell your story to the point where your message is well understood. Also remember in the course of writing your screenplay, you may have to take some days off to further create suspense and know how to use your characters effectively to tell your story.

ABBREVATIONS IN SCREEN PLAY WRITING

As a screen play writer, I will strongly suggest that you use the following abbreviations so as to save time.

1. **INT – FOR INTERIOR**

2. **EXT – FOR EXTERIOR**

3. **SC – FOR SCENE**

4. **XTERS – FOR CHARACTER** may not be necessary when writing

5. **ESTAB – FOR ESTABLISHING** (if you are indicating camera movement, although may not be necessary, as director take charge of camera movements).

6. **CAM – FOR CAMERA**- only necessary when indicating camera movements, as a fresher not necessary at all.

7. **MVT- MOVEMENT**- if you don't want to use scene to separate your screenplay.

8. **LOC – LOCATION** - may not be necessary when writing.

BUSINESS ANGLES OF STORY WRITING AND SCREENPLAY WRITING

1.   If you write a very good story, you can sell for as high as ₦50, 000 (fifty thousand naira) if you can write ten good stories within a year, you will make ₦500, 000 (five hundred thousand naira)

2.   If you can write a good marketable screenplay of the story, your fee will increase, you can earn up to ₦150,000 (one hundred and fifty thousand) per work, if you can write ten good marketable screenplays in a year, you will earn up to ₦1, 500,000 (one million five hundred thousand)

FACTS THAT CAN HELP YOU RISE TO THE TOP EASILY AS A CREATIVE WRITER AND OTHER BUSINESS ANGLES

As a creative writer, it is advisable for you to join the script writers guild of Nigeria. Before you show your script to any producer or marketer, first get your **ISBN** from the national library and get it registered with Nigeria copy right commission; these will make you command respect. If you don't have the fund to do these, you can wait till you are ready (you can make contacts on how to join the guild from national theater Lagos or other branches Nation wide). (if you are based outside Nigeria, you can make inquiry about it in your country) . Before you

39

present your work to any producer/marketer, you must ensure he likes your kind of story, so you must watch some films he has previously produced: every producer/marketers has a line of story he follows e.g. religious story, romantic thrillers, romantic adventures, love story, cultural story etc. (remember, you can combine these stories into one to make your work attractive). A producer/marketer will first request for the synopsis (synopsis is the written or verbal summary of your story) in presenting the synopsis of your story, you must not give details, give few points that you know are attractive in your story, if he is interested, you can now present your entire script either story or screenplay. Do not type your screenplay script before presenting it, because you may need to adjust it, (write clearly though) as sometimes a marketer/producer may request for such adjustment (for screenplay only). Do not insist on collecting a high fee for your first work, you can use it as a sacrifice, if your work is good and does well in the market, you will be amazed at the opportunities that will come your way. You must be creative with your title it must be one that keep people in suspense. I suggest you first start a cordial relationship first with a producer/marketer before you present your work to him; you can be calling him to praise him for his previous work, somehow find a way to start off a relationship. I strongly suggest that you engage a female marketer to help you market your works and reach a written agreement on what to pay her at least 10%.

HOW TO EASILY LOCATE PEOPLE YOU CAN WORK WITH

This is very simple just pick a jacket of already produced films, you will see the numbers with which to contact prospective marketers/producers. Some jackets even have email addresses.

If you watch most Ghana films, you will observe that Nigerians are partnering with Ghanaians to write story for them, produce, and direct the films as well as marketing them here in Nigeria and other African countries. However, as a fresher you are to start first and make impact locally before you can go for such move.

HOW TO BECOME A PRODUCER

WHO IS A FILM PRODUCER:

A film producer is akin to the managing director of any organization, he is the one who seeks for finance to get the film produced. First and foremost, he will require a completed screen play of a story to start thinking about producing the film.

FIRST STEP

Upon acquiring the story, your story must have the kind message you have in mind, to educate inform and entertain, (the cost of acquiring a story, depends on your bargaining power with the writer, or the writer you are buying from ordinarily a completed screen played story will sell from ₦150,000, if you are buying from established writer, whilst unknown writers could sell their first story for between ₦70, 000 or ₦50, 000, you can create a story, then contact a screen play writer to develop it thereafter you will call a script conference; but you must establish a contact with a good film director, he will charge you his fee he may as well link you with a notable marketer, with these two, you can organize the conference, they may decide to introduce two or three professionals in the industry, you will pay them a minimal fee; they may decide to change something in the script but everything depends on what you think about the story you want to produce thereafter you will go ahead to type the script, after typing , costing becomes easy for you first you will need a costumier he or she provides all the dresses the characters in your story will put on, then you will need a location manager, to secure locations where the film will be shot, then you will need a props man, that will provide all the props that are inside your written screen play e.g. are cars, drinks, cigarette, including any other things that the characters in your screen played story will be using in the course of shooting your film, the costing of these three sets of items depends on the screen play you have to shoot, each scene determines the cost of any of the item stated above, of course if it is a rich setting in the scene that means the costumes, the props and location will cost you high, if it is a poor setting you will pay less depending on your negotiating power, rich costumes depending on the number of characters in the scene very rich costumes per character should cost you a maximum of one thousand naira same thing is applicable to the props and also the locations. However in the case of locations, you will pay per each location a very rich location may cost as much as ₦5, 000 to ₦10, 000 some smart fellows may even charge you per each scene shot in their location i.e. if you shoot five scenes in a very rich location, you may pay as much as ₦50, 000 how ever you may just rent an hotel and pay for the number of days you will shoot your scenes this is far cheaper. For props, cars appear to be the most costly currently in our own setting, you may pay as high as ₦1, 000 per scene that a car appears in your film. These processes are known as pre production i.e. typing of the shooting script, getting your locations, your props and as well the costumes and also audition venue; audition is like the normal interview you conduct when you want to engage people for employment; in the case of audition, you put notices across at very conspicuous places inviting people for your upcoming film to be shot.

SECOND STEP

Along with your chosen film Director each of the people that will come for the audition will be given the script to read, in the course of reading the script the director will be able to choose the best for each character in your script. In most cases the known stars just come in to pick your script for rehearsals on their own before commencement of your shooting. Upon completing the audition you will have to call the chosen artistes along with the film director so that they will undergo a process of rehearsals for about 5-10days, so that they can fit into the characters in your story. Upon completing these pre-production stages you will then proceed into the production proper, this is where you really have to invest good money so as to get a very good production. Already you have a film director, with his help he will link you up with notable stars, depending on who you want and the capital you have at your disposal to invest in the film, in film making the more money you put into it the more quality you get into it, and it will in turn attract very high patronage from a marketer, that will sale your film for you to the general public. In the course of production, you will need a D.O.P. director of photography i.e. camera man you will have to hire his camera and hire him too. You will need an assistant director, who will ensure the artistes get into top shape of the characters before they face the camera. Definitely you will also need support characters that will assist your main characters in interpreting your story; there are also the minor characters, these are people that assist both your lead role characters and support characters to interpret your story, you will need a make up artist whose duty is to beautify the artistes before they appear in the front of the camera; still photographer, is the person that will snap as many pictures as possible in the course of shooting of the film, these pictures will be helpful when the jackets for the film are being made; then you will need a continuity man; his work is similar to that of a secretary, he takes note of every incidents that take place in the course of shooting of the film, his notes will guide the editor, in the course of editing the film; you will also need a bus and a driver to move you and the artistes from one location to another. A production manager is also one of those you are to engage, he is very relevant too in the course of shooting your film, he is the one that will assist you greatly in the course of shooting your film, he organizes how the film will be shot from a location to another, and also coordinate all the crew members into a team, comprising of the costumier, make up artiste, props manager, location manager, production assistants, are those that play role of moving things around in the course of shooting as well as they play the role of any other requirements on set. There is also the welfare person, he/she is the one that will prepare what the cast and crew will eat while on your set. You will need a generator to power the camera, you have to make provision to fuel the generator set.

THIRD STEP

After production, you take the recorded tape to an editor, who will edit the film, in the course of doing this the sound track will also be inserted, you however need to contract someone to do the soundtrack for you before you start shooting .Your film director can assist to link you up with a sound tracker.

BUDGET PROPOSAL FOR FILM PRODUCTION
10 DAYS PROJECTED PRODUCTION

Pre-production

Typing of script/ photocopies   ₦ 15, 00.00

Script/ scriptwriter fee   ₦150, 000.00

Audition (rent a place)   ₦ 5, 000.00

Location manager fees/ location   ₦250, 000.00

Props manager / props   ₦ 80, 000.00

Contingency for production   ₦100, 000.00

Production

Director   ₦400, 0000

Asst director   ₦ 70,000.00

Lead   artiste   ₦500, 000.00(Male)

Lead   artiste   ₦500,   000 female

Support artiste   ₦200, 000.00

Minor roles   ₦ 60,000.00 at N 2,000 per artist per   scene 30 artistes

Renting of camera/ Camera man fees ₦250, 000 10 days shooting at N 15,000 per day

N 10,000 per day for D.O.P.

Make up   ₦ 30,000

Welfare fee   ₦150, 000 10days

Feeding ₦ 10,000 per day

₦5,000 per day for welfare provider fee

Transport Bus & Driver   ₦100, 000
10 days shooting N10, 000 per day

Gen set & fuel   ₦60, 000 rent
& fuel 10 days

Continuity Man   ₦30, 000

Production Manager   ₦100, 000

Production Assistants *(4)   ₦200, 000 N50,
000 each * 10 days

Light & Soundman   ₦ 50,000

Cameraman Assistant   ₦ 50,000

Accommodation   ₦ 180,000

POST PRODUCTION

Editing   ₦ 80,000

Soundtrack   ₦ 20,000

NOTES: This out look is base on the projection of a script I wrote; if you are to Produce your film, definitely the costing of your script will be different from mine; it is very imperative for you to note also that your ability to negotiate powerfully plays a vital role in producing your film I.e. in terms of high or low budget proposal. But do not compromise on having a good quality film by costing your film too low. You may have to provide accommodation(hotel) for you, director and your lead characters base on the number of days you will shoot your film, but for the stars, ensure you shoot the scenes they are involved in first so as to reduce your hotel fee, if you are smart you can use the hotel rooms to shoot some interior scenes in your script; also shoot the exterior scenes(stars) first, if other artistes are very vital to your production, you may also need to provide hotel rooms for them too.

BUSINESS ANGLES OF FILM PRODUCTION

HOW TO EASILY MAKE IT AS A PRODUCER

I strongly advise that as a first timer you have to first and foremost register your membership after you must have register your business with corporate affairs commission with association of movie producer (AMP) the best place to easily get linked up with other producers that will easily link you up is the national theater, AMP also have branches almost in every state. However if you are based outside Nigeria you can ask around how to join film producers groups. For your first two films, I strongly suggest that you go into partnership with an established producer or director to produce them for you; this must be after you have established a very good friendly relationship with him e.g. if you have Three million naira to produce (including cost of script for your film), talk to a known director/ producer, tell him your capital include his own fee, have a written document with him to produce/direct your film and also market it to a marketer for you, remember to also reach agreement of what you want to make as profit from your film. You can reach agreement of a least of 30% return on your invested capital. Ensure that you are present all through the course of shooting your film, so that you can gradually learn all the tricks involved.

HOW TO MAKE YOUR FILM ATTRACTIVE:

Worldwide established stars make films to sale; in producing your film, it is advisable that you use one or two A listed stars for your film, an established producer/ director will advise you on the best artistes to use for your film. After partnering with a producer/ director to produce your first two works, you have to pay attention to the details of how he will produce these films, so that by the time you want to fully commence your own production, things will be easy for you

THINGS TO AVOID WHILE PRODUCING:

Naturally as a producer there is the tendency to become bossy since you are the person that seek for the capital to enable the production become a reality; but you have to be very careful while on set shooting your film, especially with your director and established stars, allow all instructions to come from the director once you are on set; if you notice any thing you do not like, call the director aside and notify him. Do not get into any quarreling bout with the stars or any body on your set. You should try as much as possible to go the extra mile to make every one happy on your set. From your contingency money you can make extra provision for the stars on your set e.g. drinks, meat pies e.t.c

TIME FACTOR:

In film production, time is very essential you must be very conscious of your time, if you are to shoot for 2 weeks ensure you stick to the time especially [the volume of your script determines how long] as it concern your investor you must tell him when he will recoup the invested capital plus profit. Capital invested can be recouped plus profit within 90 days, however you can produce within 30 days and sale outright to a marketer, this means selling your master tape to a marketer, by this process the marketer becomes the owner of the film, before you commence production that you wish to sell outright your director/producer must link you up first with the would be marketer and intimate him of your intention.

HOW TO START FILM PRODUCING ON PART-TIME BASIS:

You can produce your film on a part-time basis, if you are engage in other activities e.g. Working, you can produce your film during your leave period at least two films in a year by splitting your leave into two halves. On the other hand, if you have access to fund you can enter into a permanent agreement with an established film director / producer to produce for you(acquiring stories for you, you may indicate the type of story you want him to produce for you) quarterly with your first capital as revolving capital, and you will be reaping profit either quarterly if you want him to produce and market your works or every 30 days if you want to be selling your work out rightly to a marketer after productions.

HOW TO START PRODUCING YOUR WORKS ON PARTNERSHIP BASIS:

You can start the production of your work on a partnership basis. Upon acquiring a story of your choice, you can get some of the things that are needed to produce your work for free and tell those that will assist you, that you will pay them later, but this means you have to do a lot of talking and convincing, you may easily get these things within your area of abode, things like locations, props, and very good costumes according to the dictate of your story, then you can get some people within your area and do several rehearsals with them to play the roles of minor characters, after these processes you can approach a producer or a marketer and tell him about your efforts, with a good story and well screen played, any marketer or producer will be much interested to provide other requirements. You can then reach a mutually agreed terms on how to share the profit. You must make sure, that you put into consideration those that you will pay, as well as your own projected profit, before reaching a profit sharing formula with the marketer or producer: But you have to be on the "low side positively", because the marketer or producer can assist you further in your other works.

HOW TO START SMALL AND GROW BIG:

As a fresher, this option will be the best. In starting small you acquire a small story of say 40 scenes, then do rehearsals with unknown artistes within your area for up to 10-15 days, ensure that the people are very interested in the business, talked to a director, there after raise some small capital to get a camera and a camera man, then talk to people in your area to allow you use their houses for free, get your props within your area for free by appealing to people, the artistes you will use will help in bringing their costumes if you cannot provide them, after shooting you still need some capital to get the film edited, because it is a small work, you don't really need to go to a big editing studio. There after, get your film approve for marketing by national film and video census board; you can then market your film within your area and beyond, depending on your mobility, with the profit you realize, you can start joining the big league gradually after two or three times; remember to compensate those that assisted you in your first film(s). (You definitely have to raise some capital for jacket at least 1,000 pieces to package the mass dubbed DVD/CD which also require you to raise some capital to do this). These days YouTube has become another viable source to sell your films, you can as well explore this avenue to grow your business. If you are quite consistent you will gradually build a solid customer base with good and quality films via YouTube.

HOW TO START BIG AND MAINTAIN IT:

You can start big, if you have access to huge finance. In starting big, you will have to provide finance for the production and marketing of your work. You will have to use established artistes, director/producer. After production, the next step is marketing process including mass dubbing of the master tape, printing of jacket and posters, but as a fresher you definitely need an experience film marketer or film producer to assist you in this task(s), to arrive at a reasonable unit cost to sell to the marketer, you need your director to assist you before approaching a marketer that will market the film to the public. As stated above, you can as well use YouTube to maximize your profit. You can as well market your work to ROK TV, Amazon, Netflix etc .

PRODUCING FILMS IN YOUR LOCAL DIALECT : Some film producers are really cashing in on this, especially our friends from Yoruba, Hausa and Igbo speaking areas . They are producing films in their local dialect and are equally smiling to the banks, DSTV incidentally has channels that air this films too, so apart from marketing your films produced in your local dialect, you can as well market them via the mediums stated above and you will be making cool cash.

BELOW ARE SOME OF THE JOBS THAT ARE AVAILABLE IN NOLLYWOOD FILM INDUSTRY

PROPS MAN

A props man, is the one that provides all the items to be use as indicated in a script, typical examples of items that may be indicated in a script are cars, drinks, handbags, handsets the list is endless, a script determines the types of props i.e. items to be use in the course of shooting a film. Your fee will be determined by the cost of each props i.e. items per scene in a script setting after getting and costing the items by negotiating with owners or the ones you have, you will then go ahead to negotiate your own fee with the film producer, including the cost of the items **(Props) but** you must endeavour to be very fair in your charges, so that you don't over charge and lose the job. With adequate connections, you can be getting jobs regularity: it is also strongly advised that intending props man should try to create a good business relationship with as many film producers as possible so if you have access to props directly or indirectly that can be use in film production, Nollywood has a job for you.

LOCATION MANAGER:

Do you know people that have good and beautiful houses that can be used to produce film? Then you have a job offer in the Nollywood industry; incidentally, it is not only beautiful houses that you need to know about to become a location manager in Nollywood, as some scripts are written with poor or dilapidated houses as locations where films will be shot, some scripts can have both i.e. rich and poor locations. In doing your costing, you have to first negotiate with the owners of the houses upon being contracted by a film producer, after reaching an agreeable price with the owners of the houses, you will then approach your producer and discuss on your own fee together with the cost of the locations; always be very fair with your charges, your charges will include your cost of movements to get the locations. You maybe fortunate to use some locations you have used in a previous film for another one depending on the dictate of the script. Some smart location managers can creatively use one house to shoot many scenes.

COSTUMIER:

Are you a good fashion designer? Are you good at dressing people well as per any occasion? Do you know the right dresses for any occasion or any situation? Then you can make good money for yourself in Nollywood. All the dresses you see actors and actresses wear in films are provided for them by a costumier, who is very creative and knows what all artistes are suppose to wear base on the dictate of the script in a film setting per scene. The types of dresses you provide for the cast i.e. actors and actresses determines your cost; upon being given a script to provide costumes, you have to go out and look for these costumes and negotiate what to pay for them and then meet with the film producer to discuss the cost and your own fee, the types of costumes determines your charges, but be very fair. Some of the places to get costumes are from friends, fashion houses, family member's e.t.c. always ensure your costumes are neat or as indicated in the script.

WELFARE PROVIDER:

Can you cook good foods? Are you a professional caterer? You have jobs in Nollywood waiting for you. The script for shooting a film determines what it will cost you to provide food for the cast and (crew) as well the types of foods required i.e. the actors and actresses and others that will work on the set in the course of shooting the film. Your fee will also be determined by these factors. The film producer will inform you about the kind of foods required on set. Always be fair in your charges.

BUS DRIVER: Do you have a bus? Then you can move the cast and crew from one location to another for a fee, you charge your daily fee per day; charge what you earn daily from your normal transport business.

SOME PROFESSIONAL JOBS IN NOLLYWOOD:

The following jobs require some trainings before you can perform optimally in Nollywood.

PRODUCTION MANAGER:

As a production manager, you must be good at organizing, preparing and also time conscious. A production manager is the person who organizes and prepares everything needed in the course of shooting a film, as a result he liaise with all of the above mentioned people before the cast and crew comes on set for the shooting of the movie. He also dictates when and where a scene is to be shot; in most cases he decides the movements of the cast and crew. He also draws chart for the shooting of the films. Some smart Nigerians that have worked in many movie sets have diverted into this area of film production. Joining production managers association will enable you know what to charge.

CAMERAMAN: Are you a trained video camera man? (They are professionally called director of photography DOP) then find your way into Nollywood and make real good money for yourself. All you need is to do one very good job and you will be amaze at what that one work will do for your career in the Nollywood industry. If you join an association, in Nollywood for DOPs you will easily know your rightful fee.

SET DESIGNER: A set designer is the person who designs the set base on the dictate of the script. A set designer must have a good sense of arranging a location in a way that the cameraman will pick good angles and make a beautiful film.

STILL PHOTOGRAPHER: He is the person who uses small camera to take pictures. A still photographer is very relevant in Nollywood. In the course of shooting a film, a still photographer takes many shots of the cast, and crew in the end some of these shots taken are used to produce the jackets for the film. So if you are a trained still photographer and you need good job, Nollywood is waiting for you.

CONTINUITY MAN: The continuity man, is like a typical secretary, he takes note of all the shots taken on set and ensures that there is continuity base on the dictate of the scripts and shots taken on set, his notes act as a guide to the film editor.

SOUNDTRACKER: Are you good at composing music? Then Nollywood has job for you, as music played in films are compose by songwriters/musicians based on the story of the film.

NOTES: Adequate trainings are relevant in these stated jobs, also joining the various guilds that control these jobs in Nollywood may be helpful to easily getting jobs in Nollywood and also have the regulated fees charged by others.

MOVIE DIRECTOR: This is a highly professional job that requires some level of training before you can get into the art. You can as well learn the trade on the job if you are fortunate to meet a good movie Director or who is willing to let you know all the tricks involve in directing. Directing is actually all about knowing the right angles to use, understanding the characters in the script and be able to interpret them to those that will play them out, knowing how to direct the movement of the camera as well as taking your shots rightly and accurately. As a movie director, you are the boss on set; it is your ability to control all that happens once the camera start rolling that determines the success of the movie you are directing. However you should endeavour to have a good rapport with the producer and executive producer on location. Being a graduate (of theatre arts) will be beneficial in this art, but you may master the art through learning or training and joining the director's membership will enable you know what to charge.

ARTISTIC DIRECTOR: An artistic director is also known as assistant director. As an assistant director, you are to get the artiste into characters before they face the camera where the director calls the shots. The job of assistant director is so very essential that an intending assistant director must be of similar intelligence like the movie director. To get into the art, you have to learn it on the job or after rigorous training or through schooling. Your membership of the director's body will be of great importance to you in this trade it will also benefit you to join the membership as a movie director, so as to know what to charge.

FILM EDITOR: As a film editor, you need to get a thorough training before proceeding into this art. The film editor is the person who puts the bits and pieces of film together in a way that it becomes descent for the eyes to see as well as the ear to hear i.e. audio/visual quality, arranging also the film sequentially because films are not shot in sequentially order. If you are fortunate too you can meet someone that can teach you how to edit. Definitely, being a computer literate will make you very effective in this trade.

MAKEUP ARTISTE: Makeup artiste is another highly professional job in the Nollywood industry. As a makeup artiste you need to know more than just applying makeup on people faces, you have to be highly creative to stand out as a makeup artiste in the industry, because every script has its pattern of making up the artiste in a way that your work will be in tune with the way the writer portrays the characters in the script. If you are very passionate about this job, you can as well learn it on the job. Get into membership with the relevant bodies.

ACTING: Acting is the art of behaving in a way that maybe unusual of a person's character. In acting a person is required to play a role he/she may not be familiar with, in doing so, he must show a great deal of passion in his/her trade when called upon. There are many aspects of acting which an actor/actress may be required to perform in the course of his/her job they include lead role, support role and minor role, there is also "Waka pass": In playing the the lead role an actor/actress is used by the writer to tell his/her story in the manner he/she (the writer) feels like revealing his/her story to the understanding of his audience(s), in most cases the lead character appears from the beginning of the story to the end or plays a "large chunk" in the entire story. An actor/actress must note that playing the lead role, he or she does not have a fixed type of character to play, as stated above, the writer's angle of a story determines the way and manner a lead character will deliver on his/her trade in the course of playing the role in a film setting; of great importance too to a budding artiste to note, is the fact that each scene in a script (a script is the note written by a writer dictating how all the characters will play their roles – see my screen played script in the other pages) determines the mood of the actor/actress per scene i.e. in a particular scene an actor/actress may be required to act like a drunkard, while in another scene he/she may act like a gentleman e.t.c, in each scene the actor/actress is expected to adjust to the requirement(s) of each scene, in some scenes an actor/actress may have to combine different characters in order to tell the writer's story effectively. In some cases a lead role player, plays the role of a protagonist; in being a protagonist, the lead character plays a positive role, while in being an antagonist, the lead character is acting negatively. Some actors/actresses even go as far as studying the way a particular character behaves in real life before they go on set, after receiving the script. Another crucial point you should note as a budding actor/actress is the fact that an established actor/actress have a way to deliver his/her role when called upon e.g. if Mercy Johnson is requested to play the role of a pastor, the way she will deliver her lines will be different from the way Genevieve Nnaji will deliver her lines if given the same role, but at the end of the day the message of the writer will definitely "sink in". In playing the role of a support character, as the name implies, a support character is the one who supports the lead character to tell the story of the writer, in some cases, you have the support character playing the role of a protagonist along with the lead character, while on the other hand a support character plays an opposite role to that of the lead character i.e. as an antagonist, while the lead character plays the role of a protagonist. As stated earlier, the dictate of the script determines how a support character plays his or her role per scene. A minor character is one that plays a minimal role in a movie production. In most cases a minor character acts as backups to the lead character and support character to tell the story of the writer. As a starter you are most likely to get a minor role often when you get such opportunities do it so passionately, deliver your lines with precision and do well to get into the character you are expected to play out; do not joke with "Waka pass" role too, you never can tell what you do that can attract the interest of the director or producer e.g. your movement, your gesticulation e.t.c. before long you will start getting calls for bigger roles. Anytime you see call for audition endevour to attend, even if at the end of the day you are not chosen for any role, be persistent don't let your passion to wane.

The art of acting is like the art of writing, the more you show passion for it, the more you become good at it. When you go for audition, make sure you read your script loudly and try to put some liveliness or dullness into it, depending on the dictate of the script, get very well into the character i.e. behave so well like the character you are asked to play; take time to watch others perform, learn from them, these are some of the things that will endear you to producers/directors, also take note to be humble, friendly, do not allow people praising you to get into your head if you are good, treat everybody equally, respect those that are ahead of you in the trade, respect your director and producer they can be of immense value to your career, be good to everyone. Joining the body controlling actors/actresses will be beneficial to you.

Some terms used by the directors, that you should be familiar with as an actor/actress.

ACTION: By this term, the Director is asking you to start acting base on the dictate of the script.

CUT: By this term, the Director is asking the camera man to stop filming to correct some noticed flaws.

FREEZE: This means you should stop at the point where you are, in most cases in such situation, the

Director must have notice some flaws to correct at the point where you are or other artistes are.

PROJECT: This term means speak out, once a Director says project, it means you should raise your voice.

SET: Is the place where a particular shot will be taken at a point in time. Once you hear the Director calls for artistes on set, he is referring to all the artistes for that scene to gather at the spot where the filming will be take place.

CUE UP: The term cue up means you should take your own line after the actors/actress you are acting with has taken   his/her   own line.

SOME JOBS IN THE CREATIVE AND ENTERTAINMENT INDUSTRY THAT CAN BE DONE ON A PART /FULL TIME BASIS.

Football agents: Football is one angle of entertainment that few smart Nigerians are using to earn big money for themselves. Despite this, many are still very much ignorant that football is an entertainment sport from which they can make megabucks. If you are a good observer, you will notice that many players worldwide have agents that market them to clubs, even right here in our country it is also happening locally. You can delve into this aspect of entertainment by first obtaining a license from the appropriate authorities to market players, but you must show a great deal of passion for this job, you must know a great deal of football matters and all the business angles before applying for the license because you will have to pass an exam before the license will be issued to you, to start marketing players locally and internationally. Finance is very key in this business, you can package a mouth watering proposal of some talented footballers you have around you, then approach a money bag within your locality i.e. 70% - 30% to you, the benefit to the financier for the starting point 70%,to the financier after or before you write your exams to obtain your license, you really have to do a great deal of research. If you are very passionate about this job, this job requires a good deal of network connections, you must know agents that know coaches both locally and internationally, this will help you a lot in this business. You must have written document with your players. You must know agents too that have local and international connections.

Marketing talented artistes/actors: If you look around you within your area, you will see there are many actors/musicians that are eager for exposure, they are wasting away, do you know a film producer, or you know anybody who knows these people?, why not reach an agreement with these talented people to link them up with these producers and have your cuts from fees they will earn by being engaged by these producers? Meanwhile if you have good connections that can enable you to also connect comedians to market them to the public especially as it concerns parties, e.t.c. i.e. politicians, people that organize both formal/informal parties. Most importantly in this angle of the creative/entertainment industry is to be very patient, at the initial stage as a budding marketer of talented persons your artiste will be earning low fee, but with good performances and your vigorous marketing, your artiste will start earning big money and you will also start to earn big . Always have a written document binding you and your artistes on how you will be sharing money to accrue from the business. I strongly recommend 30% to you as the marketer because if you are very smart you will definitely have more than one artiste on your stable as a result you are most likely going to earn more from your other artistes. Get your outfit registered as an entertainment out fit with the CAC.

Sport Presentation: Are you very knowledgeable in sports matters are you a Sport Historian, do you know about sports men and women, their achievements, success stories, failures e.t.c., and also very fluent in the use of English language, can you spice it up with some "flavours" or comedy? e.t.c and on consistent basis then of course the Creative / entertainment business has got job for you and good money for you to make. All you actually need to do is to get yourself "brushed up" on how to present sports on radio / television then join membership of sports to facilitate your growth in this business. After your training on presentation, you should be able to write an attractive proposal to interested outfits, that will easily jump at such opportunity so as to enable them as well to advertise and promote their products, services, ideas etc to the public. I tell you honestly, if you can get into this job, the sky will be your starting point. I recommend that you firstly go into collaboration with those that have made name in this field, this will ensure easy success in this business after sometime you can start presenting on your own. Being a graduate may be an advantage in this business of sport presentation.

You can as well do this job in your local dialect if you are very fluent in it; some smart people especially our Yoruba, Igbo and Hausa brothers are making money presenting sports in their local dialects. Another appealing aspect is to create a signature tune (song) that will be played in the beginning and the end of your sports presentation also know that you will buy airtime from the radio / televisions stations include this cost in your proposal to interested firms.

If you are a money bag and know somebody that is talented in this art, you can finance such talent to do this business, you can reach concrete agreement on what to pay him/her either weekly or monthly. Also get your outfit registered with CAC. Voice training will be beneficial for you in this business.

Be a party entertainer: You can actually put up some creative stuff within your locality, especially during festive periods. You can think of creative ways to entertain people base on what you feel can appeal to your people within your locality. I have seen handicap persons entertain people at parties and they are sprayed good sums of money, I have seen a group of young boys and girls entertain people in parties with good dance steps, they are contracted for parties by organizers get paid and yet also get sprayed in the party, I have seen a group of young boys and girls entertain people in parties with good dance steps, they are contracted for parties by organizers get paid and yet also get sprayed in the party, I have also seen on several occasions groups that have local musical instruments entertaining people in parties and making good money for themselves, the list is endless, you can just think up a creative way to entertain people and continue practicing it till you become a master of the art (either yourself or with a group). You can even carve a niche for yourself in this area of creative /entertainment business by creating periods to organizing shows within your locality. Some smart Nigerians use the period of their Communities annual celebrations and make good money in the process. Some Nigerians have different types of occasion as well as different forms of entrainment for marriage ceremonies, burial ceremonies, coronation ceremonies etc to display their arts; some have become house holds names within their localities and beyond to the point that they are usually invited and paid well for shows

Music Director: As in film directing, the same thing is applicable to music directing, however as a music director, you must have a good sense of dance steps, good sense of using the camera to tell the story of the musician /songwriter, a good sense of using dance steps to entertain and as well tell the story of the song.

Songwriting: All the songs you hear are written by someone. Songwriting is one lucrative business you can go into. Songwriting is like poem writing, however in songs writing you have to be lucid, your words should be easily comprehended, unlike in poems where many allusions are use. If you can write songs that can stand out and become a success in the market place then be sure you will earn megabucks.

How to write your song: Before you think of writing a song, you must first and foremost have a story in mind, after developing the story in your mind, you will then have to be more creative to write out the lyrics in a way that you will still maintain the angle of your story; you can use different angles, perhaps deviating from your story angles, but in the end, you must come back to the message you are passing across. Your song must contain a chorus: a chorus is the lines that are most often repeated by the artiste in the course of singing the song, most often than not, the songwriter uses the chorus to effectively pass the message across.

My song title – Deeply in love

1st stanza - *I remember seeing your face long time ago, I tried to express my deep feelings then, but I found it so hard to do so, now seeing you again, the feeling is building up again and again,*

Chorus: *o baby girl, I am so deeply in love,*

so very much deeply in love with
you,

this time, I can't hold it back,

this time, I won't let the opportunity slip
again,

I am so deeply in love with you.

2nd stanza -   *o baby girl, you are my love*

o darling, I am so happy to see you
again,

3rd stanza -   *my heart is filled with joy,*

o my love, no matter what they say or do

they can't stop me from loving
you,

I am all yours now.

NOTES: If you take a careful look at my lyrics you will notice that it is strongly laced with romantic words consequently as the lyricist I will advise the artiste to sing the song at a slow pace with a lot of passion, so that my message will be well comprehended; as a result when you are writing the lyrics of your song you must try to know the tempo which your song will better flow with; things that determine the tempo that will decide how your song will flow are what did you see ?, what did you hear? What motivated you into writing the song?, all of these or one of them will determine the tempo of how your song will flow . Your song can also come from your personal experience.

Business angles; your joining of membership of musicians / song writers association will be of tremendous help you to easily get your song out to artistes / music producers. Get your written song registered with relevant authorities to have your copyright protection. To get those to easily work with, just get jackets of produced songs and you will see addresses and telephone numbers of many producers & musicians, but you have to make sure the producer / musician must be the type that like the kind of your written songs, because producers / musicians like particular lyrics of songs e.g. R & B, highlife, romantic, gospel songs etc some also like a blend of different songs patterns i.e. you can actually combine R&B and gospel songs. I strongly advise you to find a way to build a good relationship with a producer / musician before presenting your work i.e. phone calls, face book, twitter, face to face talk are strong ways to build a relationship. If you know anyone that is close to the producer / musician, you can approach the person to link you up.

As a fresher don't be too conscious of money, try to do good songs if you write good song that ends up doing well in the market, then be sure you will get many producers / musicians knocking on your door to write songs for them. Have it at the back of your mind that many producers / musicians are also into songwriting so for you to be able to convince them with your own songs, you must do very excellent works. Do not just write only one song and rush to sell it to a producer / musician, if you are observant, you will notice that most produced albums have many songs, so try to write as many as six songs before presenting them for consideration by a producer/musician. It will do you no harm if you use your first sets of good written songs as "sacrifice" to launch yourself into the business. If you are financially buoyant or have access to fund, you can organize musical talent shows in your locality in collaboration with some experts in the business so as to discover fresh talents, then link the talents with good and notable music producer[s] to produce your written song; you can as well make the talents you discover, in your shows to do a "collabo" with notable musicians, to produce your written songs using notable music producers. However, you have to be careful don't just jump into production, a lot goes into it, you have to understand the rudiments and gradually build upon it before you finally approach a producer to produce your works into music, in no time, if you are patient enough and also a fast learner, you can start producing yourself . Your producer is definitely going to add his own creativity to your lyrics , so as to make your songs commercial success. Consider engaging a pfemale marketer to market your songs and at least pay her a certain percentage of your fee, have a binding agreement.

RULES TO ADHERE TO WHEN SONGWRITING

1.   Develop a story either from what you hear, read and see, or from a personal experience have a strong passion for the story. There must be a message in your story.

2. Create words to form the lyrics of your songs

3.   Use words that are effective to the message you want to pass across to   develop the lines of your song

4.   Write in sequential lines

5.   Separate your lines with comma at end of each lines end it with a full stop after the lines per each stanza

6.   Write in stanza (you can see my model)

7.   You can write up to 3 or more stanzas

8.   Your chorus should come after your first stanza, although it is not a rule, consequently, your chorus can come after the 1st or 2nd stanza, depending on how you feel about the song you are writing.

9.   Songs can be use as a tool of informing, entertaining or educating, your story angle and lyrics should go along with these points of views or you can combine two or three of these points of views to pass your message across, but essentially and as stated before do not loose the import of your line of thought i.e. your message.

CREATE A PROGRAM FOR RADIO OR TV:

Just like in sport presenting, you can create a programme for radio or TV depending on the capital that you can use such programme to attract from corporate bodies that will be ever willing to sponsor a well articulated programme. First and foremost, you must be passionate about an idea, you must have a field of specialization, and you must be able to create a content/solution to problems that are existing in your area of specialization, which many may be feeling the negative effect without knowing the way out. like I stated in sports presentation, you can go for training on presentation, after learning the ropes on presentation, you are good to go, just package your content and write an attractive package to potential corporate bodies especially those that have interest in the content you have packaged either directly or indirectly, write to many as you can, but you first need one to get started either through the radio or TV medium. Buying a slot on TV is of course more expensive, your proposal must include the cost of buying a slot through any of the mediums and your own professional fee; be very considerate with your own fee. I know it very well that once you are established in this business, the real megabucks will start rolling in for you, corporate bodies will be ever willing to pay you your deserve fee. Also note that you should not stop at what you know in your field of specialization, go for more trainings get to know new ideas, so as to further develop your content and become a seasoned specialist in your field they will definitely make you command more respect from your sponsor(s). Voice training will also add to your value in this business. If you have finance and know anybody who is talented in this field, do not hesitate to sponsor such person, I can tell you confidently you will not regret doing this especially if you do it the right way (see my advise in the sport presentation portion). You can as well get into a concrete agreement with a marketing firm(s) to market you to prospective sponsor(s) and conclude on what commission to pay the firm(s) (this is strongly recommended).

WRITING OF CREATIVE PLAYS:

Writing of plays is one angle of the creative /entertainment business that you may consider delving into. Just like screenplay writing, plays are also written in the same manner; in playwriting, you write in a book format. If you have link to education authorities, your written play can be use in schools. Writing children plays is not a bad idea.

BUSINESS ANGLES

Register your play and obtain ISBN before pushing it into the market. All the "tricks" involve in creative screenplay writing are what you need to get into creative playwriting, just be passionate about your creative story, then go ahead to put your thought down in a play format. If you don't have finance, you can approach a financier or publishing house to publish your play via the internet, in this regard, you will need an expert. Internet is cheaper than going for direct publishing.

MAGAZINE PUBLICATION

Are you a graduate of any discipline? or are you very good in your field? Can you effectively create solutions to problems that are bedevilling people in your area or specialization? Why not consider going into magazine publication? All you need to get into this business is either to go for a short course in any of the journalism schools around or you team up with graduates of mass comm., tell them about your intentions, get a prototype of the magazine and take it to people that are financially capable to support you or you can approach a finance house to finance your magazine business; with an attractive proposal, you will easily get support for this business. In the business of magazine you may sell it within your locality, state or nationally, it depends on your outlook and finance you can attract, in your magazine, you have to add other interesting angles to it, so as to attract patronage from other persons, not just dwelling only on your main thrust i.e. creating solutions to problems in your area of specialization. note that you have to obtain your ISSN from the right authority for your magazine, you can get this after your first publication, you take your first published magazine to the authority, and you will be issued as ISSN. Register your outfit. Give a permanent and very appealing title to your magazine as per the dictate of your concept. Depending on how you want your magazine to be sold either regionally or nationally determine how you will market it. Definitely, you are to engage marketers to market your magazine around. You can as well market your magazine to corporate firms, so that they will advertise through your magazine, having your magazine in the internet will help you attract adverts too. You can attract advert patronage from individuals too.

You can sell your magazine / newspaper online and be making cool cash as well from Google.

WRITING OF MANUAL/ BOOK

What profession do you belong to? Are you good at it? Why not put together some information you know very well about in form of a manual/ book creating solutions to problems you know about in your profession. I tell you, you will be helping so many people to find solutions to problems that have been bedeviling them. Moreover this business is very lucrative, all you need to do, is to be a solution provider, and as a starter don't be too money conscious, be quite reasonable with your charges when putting your manual/ book persons have been unfaithful in this business, by trying to either steal ideas of others or promising potentials customers what they don't know anything about. So be sure you know

78

what you are writing about, so that if anyone calls you about your manual/book, you can confidently discuss wholeheartedly about what you have written. I will strongly advise that you seek for collaboration with notable media house(s) for your manual/book garner respect in the eyes of the public so that it can do well in the market place. Selling your work to the public require you to have a functional bank account but as stated above, go into partnership, ensure the bank account where your prospective buyers will pay into should be in partnership with your partners, this will also make your work command its deserve respect.

You can sell your manual via the email medium to your prospective buyers, but be very careful using this medium, so that you don't lose your idea so easily I.e. your buyers could transfer your idea(s) to friends via the same medium, thereby making your to lose money in the process. Get enough prospective buyers on your email platform before you start sending your worker(s) to your prospective buyers. Obtain ISBN for your manual. You can also sell your ideas via the kindle publishing platform, but you need an expert to do this for you. There are some membership bodies coordinating the activities of people in this business, you will do well joining any.

CREATIVE ARTICLE WRITING:

Are you good with the use of words? Can you write creatively in a play format and send across a strong message to the generality of the people? Then why not try going into creative article writing for either a newspaper house or magazine publishing outfit. If you quite absorbed all the details / highlighted in my creative screenplay writing art, then you can actually be a creative article writer. As a creative article writer, all you need to do is to write creatively screenplay wise [but in this platform it is simply call a play] on a current affairs, just pick any topic of things that are happening in the society and be very passionate about it, use very catchy titles build characters around your story and go ahead and creatively build dialogues for your characters, play your characters around, maintain the storyline and the message you want your readers to imbibe. If you can get hold of Dr. Reuben Abati's works (in the guardian of some years back) they will help to build your confidence in this creative industry line of business. In this creative industry line of business, as a budding creative article writer you have to exercise a lot of patience to become known, you have to write some creative articles for free, may be to a particular media house. If you are consistent with your write up(s) and you become well known to readers at least once week you will become hot cake to readers, the media house will have no choice than to employ you and pay you handsomely too. Some people may fancy your pattern of writing and may as well want to make a statement to the public with their own thoughts, they will hire you to write for them, and even corporate firms may buy out your page, if you can attain any of these heights, I tell you honestly you have "arrived seriously". You can help yourself by marketing your page to corporate firms or use marketers for an agreed fee.

SOME POINTS OF VIEWS THAT I SUGGEST YOU CAN BUILD YOUR CREATIVE ARTICLES AROUND

I*ronically*, you can write this way by contradictorily writing about something happening in the society i.e. writing indirectly, *euphemistically*, with this pattern you will be using pleasant words to describe your thoughts using your characters, *satirically*, as a *satirist*, you write in a way mocking foolish or absurd policies, your write up should be comically in this regard, *rhetorically* in this pattern you use impressive words to play out your thoughts using your characters and the dialogues to pass your message across (in any of the pattern you use apply this to achieve your aim). The pattern you choose is determined by the topic you are writing on, what you want to achieve with your write up, what you want your readers to learn from it i.e. ironically, satirically, rhetorically or euphemistically.

CARTOONIST:

A cartoonist is an artiste who uses his/her art works to pass strong message across to the public. As a cartoonist, you have many topics on a daily basis, from where you can pick a topic and use your cartoon to send a message to your readers. As a cartoonist you use graphics to express your thoughts. I call cartoonist parodists i.e often cartoonists tend to do mockery of things that are happening around while in the process they are passing a strong message. This creative / entertainment business angle is one good job a good artiste can delve into and make money. As a cartoonist, you can work in an electronic media house or print media in particular or independently. You can also pick your pattern from any of the point of views mentioned above. You can as well do a comic strip, by using your art and tell a story sequentially using my screenplay writing style.

EXECUTIVE PRODUCER:

Another simple name for Executive Director is Ep. As an Executive Director you provide all the finances needed for the production of a movie/music. A script / songs without finance to make it become a reality is like a mere wishful thinking or winking in the dark, as a result the executive producer plays a very crucial role by providing the much needed "steel" to ensure that a script / songs sees the light of the day. The difference between the producer and executive producer is that the producer source for fund, while the executive producer is the person who has the needed fund readily available.

Investing in Nollywood/Music and as well as in the creative and entertainment industry is a great source for getting huge returns on your investment, if the right steps are taken (see details in the producer portion in this manual). As a budding EP, do not rush into directly producing your movie/music but endeavour to learn the ropes, take time to go on location when you are investing your capital, gradually you will start by first learning the basic, if you are very patient and a fast learner, you will grab all the details of productions in movie/music. If you have fund readily available, invest in the movie/music productions as well as the creative and entertainment industry. If for instance you have ₦1million to ₦5million for small /big productions you can approach a movie /music/ producer, negotiate for at least a 30% RoI (return on investment) for a start; in Nollywood you can invest and get your RoI within 90 days i.e 3 Months; but before you approach any producer to invest your capital ensure you have establish a good relationship with him/her, directly or indirectly, ensure you have a face to face interactions many times, ensure he /she is registered with the move/music associations, have a legally binding agreement with him/her. As an Ep by investing in Nollywood/ Music Industry or the creative / entertainment industry, you will be creating jobs for so many persons and making good money i.e. returns on your investment. You can use your business outfit, you can use your film / music productions to publicize your outfit using its name as Ep in the Jackets etc.

DISCO JOCKEY

Are you fluent in the use of English, can you flow very well, presenting your thoughts to an audience? Do you know how to play and mix songs delightfully to suit any occasion, then you can actually be a DJ i.e Disco Jockey in the creative entertainment business, this job has suddenly become a very lucrative one, you can work independently or in a radio or TV station, hotels, club houses e.t.c. To add more to your talent you can go for trainings on presentation and improve your voice. You can also learn on the job by understudying good DJS. Starting off independently is your surest bet to stardom especially within your locality; I am sure you know of some persons already doing this business in your area. You can stand out by printing complimentary cards and distribute to many individuals, corporate firms, government agencies, so that once they have any ceremony, they can call on you to serve as a DJ. If you are very smart, you can as well add emceeing (MC) into your deejaying (DJ). Emcee (MC) is all about coordinating an event effectively. All the information you need to be an effective MC will be given to you by the organizer(s) of the event, then you go ahead to creatively add some flavours, some Emcee (MC) and disco jockeys latterly add comic relief to their works. If you are consistently good in your work, you could land a lucrative permanent contract with a corporate firm or government, state or federal. You can as well get a job permanent, while you still work independently as a DJ/MC. Studying the methodology of established DJS/EMCEES will help you immensely to be a success in this creative/entertainment industry business. If you don't have finance to start off i.e. to buy instruments needed to become a DJ, you can hire from established DJS, ask from them what they charge as a fresher you can charge lesser, as you grow in the business, you can bring your charges to par with theirs. The best places I suggest you start your Dejaying/Emceeing is children parties, your worship centre, events organized by your friends/your relations, your confidence will definitely grow before getting into the bigger stages. Just like in all the jobs mentioned in this manual, joining a body controlling the activities of Dejays/Emcees within your locality will be of tremendous advantage to you, if there is no such association in your area, you can team up with some like (Dejays/Emcees) minds to start an association, at least 5 dejays/emcees are enough to start an association, register with the CAC (corporate affair commission in your state). Interestingly, it is not only those that are fluently in English language that can do this job; some Dejays/Emcees are smiling to the bank doing this job in their local dialects, your ability to speak English language with your local dialect fluently will just be great for you in this job. Have a good network of important personalities, solidify your relationship with them, be very appreciative to people that link you up, (however this can only be possible if you have made a remarkable progress in the job), you have to know what each personalities that link you up want some prefer gifts to money; if you can get the "right mix" I tell you honestly, you can easily rise to the top in this creative/entertainment job. Some established Dejays/Emcees even attract persons and important dignitaries to an occasion; mere seeing their names in an invitation card is enough to "drag" a large crowd to an occasion/event; if you can get to this level then be sure, of earning real good money.

A good and established DJ working with a radio station TV or club houses or hotels, has a good solid relationship with many establish stars both in the movies and music industry; this kind of relationship often translate to business connections and money in the pocket for the Dejay (most especially with the musicians) once you get into this art (DJ/MC) and became a master of it, you will see how it works; some musicians will even approach you for worthwhile deals. Work with local talents in your locality, sell them to the outside world and grow with them, of course this means you will be making money as well from them, have a solid binding agreement with these local stars.

SOME TECHNIALITIES USE BY MOVIE/ MUSIC DIRECTORS

Some technicalities you will use in order to effectively do a good job as a movie/music Director. A good Director will do his homework very well before going on set, once on set he starts putting his creative thoughts into his work scene after scene, a written short notes will not be a bad idea for a Director going on set, while some Directors go as far as doing additional screen plays to add to that of the writer, so that they do not forget the "ingredients" they wants to add to their work

(1) **Long shot**: This is usually the first shot taken in the course of shooting, whereby the camera man takes a long shot of the characters/ items/ environment e.t.c as described by the scriptwriter i.e. this involve taken a far distance

shot by the camera man (D.P.O.) of the character/items/environment e.t.c.

(2) Medium shot: In the case of the medium shot, the Director directs the cameraman to move to a middle position, whereby he (the camera man) takes a medium shot at the characters/ items/ environment e.t.c.

(3) Close up: As the name implies, this shot is taken from a close range /position of the characters / items / environment as the writer sees it in his script i.e the cameraman (D.O.P.) moves so very close to the characters /items/environment so as to have a very close up situation of the characters / items / environment.

(4) Close up on the characters: Some Directors also do a close up on each character, with the character delivering just his/her lines alone one after the other with the cameraman so very close to the characters

Beautification of work: As Director, you have to be creative, you must add your own flavours to what the writer have written, especially by using the camera optimally i.e You use the camera effectively by taking shots of beautiful scenarios e.g beautiful houses, fine looking cars, fine shoes worn by characters, the list is endless, and it depends on the creativity you want to add into the work; moreover it is not mandatory to use beautiful things only in your work; the kind of story you are directing will determine the kind of scenarios you will use.

HOW TO BECOME A NOVELIST

PROLOGUE:

Novel writing is the art of writing down account of events as they occurred in the eyes of the writer. Novel writing can as well be formidably described as the art of creating a story by the writer using characters and situations to narrate events as he/she sees them in his/her subconscious mind; In other words, novelists in most cases imagine things happening in his/her mind and put them down (by writing) or someone that an event occurred in his/her presence may decide to put them in writing as the events began and how the events ended; In both cases i.e. either writing from subconscious mind or writing down of events, the writer must be able to make the readers of his/her story to learn something from what he/she is writing on and in most cases a writer does not only make a reader to learn something, he/she also make sure he entertains and informs the readers of the story. In entertaining the readers, a novelist applies many methods e.g. violence, sex, religious angle, cultural angle, political angle, thuggery angle, to mention a few. In informing his/her readers, a novelist uses things that are occurring around him/her or even from abroad to inform the readers e.g. Nepa, business activities, family problems (how to tackle them), lovers issues etc, it is also imperative to state here that a novelist can combine the entertaining and information (point of views) (Povs) to achieve his/her aims i.e. the novelist can use the examples stated above for entertaining pov to inform the readers and vice versa, there is no special principle guiding a novelist to entertain and inform the readers but the above examples can serve as yardsticks to inform and entertain: a novelist can create other situations to inform and entertain his/her readers depending on the story the novelist is writing about, the mood of the novelist story can as well determine what angle he/she is to entertain and inform the readers, but the novelist must not be too elaborate when informing or entertaining his/her readers, so that he/she does not get carried away and lose the import of the story he/she is writing about. A novelist must get a good grasp of the situations and characters he/she is using to write the story e.g. a novelist must know how a mad man behaves or how a king behaves or a prostitute, Pastor, or armed robber etc., he/she does not have to under go any of the experiences of any of the characters to be able to create them, but by listening to others and seeing others can enable a novelist to easily create these characters. The same thing is applicable in the case of creating situations, however they must be believable i.e. the characters and situations a novelist use to narrate the story must be seen to be real. On the other hand if a novelist wants to write down an event that occurred, if he/she was not present when the event occurred, asking questions around will be the best option, so that he/she can get a good grasp of both the characters and situations so as to easily write them down, however a novelist can combine both a true life story i.e.

event that happened in his/her presence or by asking questions around with a story he/she creates.

HOW TO CREATE A STORY FOR NOVEL

World Wide most novelists create a story and then go ahead to develop the story into different dimensions; In order to achieve his/her aim. Before a novelist starts thinking about creating a story, he/she must have a mission to achieve, there must be a strong message he /she wants to pass across, so that those that will read the novel must learn something after reading the novel. A novelist must be a good listener and /or a voracious reader. A novelist can pick a line from reading another story by another writer, but must ensure he/she does not imitate the story he/she can also listen and grab a line from someone talking, from both cases a novelist can develop a story, and then build characters and situations upon which he/she will create his/her story in different dimensions, informing, entertaining and making sure that his story has a strong message that readers will clearly understand and learn something(s) from reading it.

As a novelist every word you hear or read should arouse your interest, if you really fancy the word or words, you can instantly start creating a story from the word or words. For instance, the term "deeply in love" sound very interesting to me, upon hearing such statement as a novelist i can begin to imagine a young man and a young lady that are deeply in love, in order to create suspense, entertain and inform my readers, i will first start the narration by introducing how my characters (the young man and young lady) met, after a little while I will delve into letting my readers know how it was difficult for my characters to eventually achieve the love they wanted for themselves. I will introduce how both of them initially fell in love with other individuals against their wishes, I will narrate to my readers how one of the main characters either the young man or young lady parents fought tooth and nail to ensure that the relationship did not see the light of the day, before I will eventually round off my story by stating clearly how they (the young man and young lady) finally weathered the storm, simply because they were indeed deeply in love; a story like this depicts the act of perseverance in the face of stiff obstacles, and in the end triumphing over all oppositions and obstacles.

RULES TO ADHERE TO WHEN CREATING A STORY FOR NOVEL

1.   A novelist must have a strong passion for the story he is writing about.

2.   You must write your story sequentially by using chapters e.g. chapter I, chapter 2 etc.

3.   You should be able to describe your characters to your readers e.g. heights, looks, body structure etc, but it is not necessary that you do these all through your story, the same thing is applicable to the situations.

4.   As a novelist, you are the costumier, makeup artiste, and the director of your characters i.e. when writing your novel, you may need to describe the dresses your characters are putting on especially your main characters (costumier), you may describe the kind of makeup your characters are wearing on their faces and or hair do or haircuts, manicure and pedicure etc. (makeup), you must be able to let your readers into the mind of your characters, what they are feeling and or they are thinking about in your novel (directing). By doing these, you are as well entertaining and informing.

5.   A novelist must create dialogues for his characters, the story and situations you are writing about enables you at every point in your novel to create dialogues for your characters i.e. if you are writing a love story, you definitely should know how lovers relate to themselves, but because you will also need to create different dimensions and other characters into your story so as to create suspense, (either from entertaining or informing pov) you will need to create different dialogues, for instance, those that will be against (antagonists) your main characters, will use harsh language against the main characters, just like in real life; dialogues changes one's view and or could change one's facial expression and or could lead to negative or positive action(s) and or reaction(s) .i.e. the novelist uses dialogues to transform his/her characters.

6.   There are 3 types of characters you use to narrate your story , lead Characters (main characters), in most cases a novelist uses a male and female as his/her lead

characters although it is not a rule, but most times a novelist easily flow with a male and female as his/her lead characters, it is relevant to state here that it also does not necessarily mean that you have to use a male and female, it could be one of the two or three or may be more, everything boils down to the story and the message you want to pass across. There is also the support characters: they are the ones that serve as backups to the lead characters, so as to achieve his/her target, sometimes the novelist uses the support characters to antagonize or propagate the lead characters, it all comes down to the story the novelist is telling and what the story wants to achieve. There is also the minor characters they are the ones the novelist uses minimally to serve both the lead characters and support characters so as to further make it easier for him/her (novelist) to achieve his/her target. A novelist may see need to use different minor characters per chapter to narrate the story. It is imperative to state that lead characters are not always protagonist in a story, but because a novelist must leave a strong message, as antagonists lead characters must pay for their acts i.e. a wicked person must pay for his/her atrocities. In another way, a novelist can as well use a minor character to play a vital role in the story e.g. there is a top secret unknown to every body in the story, the lead characters and support characters are all searching for the top secret, then suddenly a minor character turns up and "blows the lid off". Protagonist is not meant only for the lead characters, neither is antagonist meant for support characters only, your message will guide you on where to put your characters into the body of the story.

7.   You must give names to your characters, and they must be names that are known to your readers. You are at liberty to name some cities or states and or community in your story, to describe your situations.

8.   Your mechanical accuracy is very vital when writing your novel.

9.   Always entitle your novel, and make it one that will not easily tell your story.

10.   Use quotation marks to indicate the dialogue of your characters e.g. "I suddenly discovered that they are deeply in love". Also remember to indicate the feelings of your characters after each dialogue you create for them. Sometimes you can neglect this. (This is the art of directing your characters as indicated before just like in film setting).

11.   Most times, when you are writing a novel, you are recounting past issues or even if you are creating a story, try to express your situations in past tense, while your dialogue should be in present tense, depending on the incidents that leads to the dialogue. Try to indicate where your characters are e.g. inside the house, outside or any where you create for them, in film parlance it is called locations.

HOW TO PREPARE FOR WRITING YOUR NOVEL

If you want to write about an event in a novel format, if the event occurred right in your presence, you can start off by recalling in totality as the events unfolded, write down all the activities, first in rough sheets, there after you may see need to add some creative angles of your own to the story especially if the events are not "big" enough to make the content of a novel, as a result, you can take some days (5days at most) to think about how you can fuse these two angles together i.e. the events and your creative angles in a way that you can you still maintain the message you want to pass across, by the 6th day you can start off putting your story down, everyday you should be able to create 5chapters in 10days you would have written 50chapters,(as a starter you can start by writing one page per chapter or it could be less) , which is enough to make a novel; however, it could be less than 50 but not less than 29 chapters; I must add that there is no principle or rule stating that you must write these numbers of chapters, so far you are able to pass your message across. If on the other hand you are creating a story of your own, once you get an interesting angle to develop a story from, take 3 days to think about how to use your characters and situations to build your story upon, always remember that suspense makes your readers see your story more interesting e.g. like in my story "deeply in love" I can first make my readers to see how my lead characters fell in love seemingly , all of sudden I will take off their minds totally from the love angles and start telling my readers the terrible obstacles they faced, I will also inform and entertain them by adding other activities they were involved in e.g. in the office, at home etc. before eventually rounding off.

It is also important to state that if you so wish, you may decide to take more than the number of days stated above to write your novel, especially if you are engaged by other activities i.e. you can create one chapter per day. Remember you must have a strong passion for the message you are passing across, remain concentrated on developing your characters to enable you tell your story with ease and your message well assimilated by your readers.

A BRIEF WRITE UP ON MY CREATED STORY TITLED "DEEPLY IN LOVE"

Chapter 1

It was a wet Thursday morning, the road leading to the national stadium was flooded. It rained heavily two hours before James left home. James Ugochuckwu was driving the new model Prado Jeep, this model had an inbuilt television and a DVD player, as he was driving along the wet road James decided to play a cool romantic music, the pictures were also showing on the television screen as the music was playing, but he decided not to watch the pictures so as to concentrate on his driving; his father had warned him to avoid watching video film while driving, to avoid accident.

After driving for about 20minutes through the flooded area, and seeing that there was a bigger flood to drive pass, he changed his mind, and diverted straight into a street; the street was inhabited by the poor and low class citizens, within 2minutes of diverting into the street he noticed a very sexy lady walking down the street swaying her rear as she walked, as he drove close to the lady the picture of his course mate while he was in the university over whelmed him, he thought in his mind that the lady looked every inch like Janet his course mate, as he drove passed her, he turned and caught a quick glimpse of her face, lo and behold, it was indeed Janet the lady he was thinking about, he quickly parked the jeep blocking her, she was walking towards him too, but her countenance did not show she knew him, so he felt he was probably mistaken her for Janet, but he decided to accost the lady. "Excuse me are you not Janet" she took a good look at him instantly it occurred to her that she knew him." Yes you are James" they hugged passionately "what a surprise I was just talking about you and Mabel the other day" James was obviously elated "wow James, you are not looking bad at all" she was always enchanted by James's good looks and body frame (he had obviously added more muscles) right from when they were in the university, "Thank you. You still have your exquisite looks," James revealed, incidentally he too had always admired her while they were in the university, but they never expressed their thoughts to each other, "Thank you too. Is that your car"? Janet was obviously over whelmed by the sheer sight of the beautiful looking car, "yes my father bought it for me as a special gift after he promoted me" James responded, "it is beautiful" Janet finally let her heart out about the car, " Thank you. So how is life with you"?

James asked, but this question seemed to have burst the bubble her facial expression changed she became utterly sober "James, it has not been easy, in fact I am just going to get money from a relation, for my siblings to use to feed" she said her response really affected James, he showed concern on his face, "Don't worry things will be okay if you believe in God, mean while come let me give you some money". They both walked to the car, James opened the door and brought out a huge sum of money and gave to her, she was very happy as she received the money. "come in let me take you back home," "what about the place you are going"?, Janet was surprise at his offer to take her in his car, "am not going to any where particularly I am just driving around the area" They both entered the car.

Chapter 2

James was from a very rich home; his father was one of the most powerful ministers in the country at that time. The following day after meeting Janet, he was sitting inside their beautiful and expensively furnished sitting room along with his mother "mum yesterday I met my former school mate after 7years of our graduation" James was obviously very happy "you sound so happy talking about this your schoolmate, who is she"? his mother had a knack for reading his mind this time she was sure, her son was up to something, "her name is Janet, mum you need to see her, she is so beautiful" James happily replied, "is her parents known within the corridors of power"? His mother was rightly sensing a strong feeling on her son's part about the lady, he felt his mother was about spoiling his fun, "mum why are you asking if her parents are known within the corridors of power"? He queried his mother, "you are my son; I can see you are falling in love with her or may be you are actually in love with her"? She further asked, "Actually mum I want to ask her for a solid relationship" "then she must come from such background to fall in love with you" "But mother is it compulsory that she must come from such background"? James not happy asked "very compulsory my dear she must be from such background, or something similar to that" she was looking serious, "mum just wait to see her first, before you talk of background I believe when you see her, you will like her"

Chapter 3

James father's house was a massive building, in fact it could be described as a master piece of some sort; within the area it was situated, it was an outstanding edifice with all the paraphernalia of modern touch here and there .

Three days after Janet and James met, Janet came to visit James on his invitation. James had specifically asked his parents to wait to see her. They were all seated in another richly decorated part of James's family house. "mum and daddy this is Janet the lady I told you we attended the same university' James was happy introducing Janet to his parents, "wow what a beautiful lady, Janet you are welcome, James has made so much noise about you" his mother who was equally a stunning beauty could not but admire Janet, even though she was pretentious about it, because she had assessed Janet as not up to standard. " Quite deservedly, James is so proud talking about you" his father too was enchanted by Janet's beauty, "Thank you very much sir, thank you very much ma" Janet reacted very shyly. James stood up,

"Janet please excuse me let me get you something to drink" James left the room "so my daughter what is your father's name? James's mother inquired from Janet, " Dickson Okolo" she replied, " Dickson Okolo that name does not ring a bell" James father was surprise, " I have never heard that name before" his wife toed his line, intentionally to add salt to injury so as to achieve her aim, " my dear, so where did your father work, or is he still working"? James's father further questioned Janet, "Actually my father worked with old public work department as a gateman, he is retired now", Janet managed to respond with a voice not sounding like her own she was feeling very embarrassed by the questions, "what? And you want to go out with my son"? James's mother reactions was more like someone who saw a ghost, she was indeed very shocked, "This is unbelievable how on earth can James do this"? James's father shook his head dejectedly and affirming his support for his wife's stance on the matter, at this juncture, Janet was feeling terribly embarrassed, James returned back to the room holding a can of juice drink; the room had some of the items inside it imported while others were exquisitely made in Nigeria they all looked so beautiful and simply out of this world. James was quick to notice the frown on Janet's face, "Janet what is the matter"? He was looking at her surprise, but she was mute, James glanced at his parents "James what do you want from this girl"? His father asked, "Dad what sort of question is that"? James was surprise, "Didn't I ask you the same question the other day"? His mother threw another question at him; Janet stood up, head bowed and walked out, "what is the meaning of this dad and mum, it is not fair, why have you embarrassed my guest,"? James was obviously sad, "James get it right, if she is just your guest, no problem however if you want to go out with her, she is not the type" his father tried to dissuade his mind from falling in love with Janet, "Dad this is just not fair" James said as he rushed outside, but Janet was gone away, he looked very unhappy, annoyingly muttering incomprehensible words.

Chapter 4

Few days after Janet visited; James and his father were sitting at an exquisite angle in front of their beautiful and mighty mansion. James looked every inch like his very handsome father, at 28, James was as tall as his 52years old father they both stood at 6feet 6inches tall, they had very sexy eyeballs, the only difference between them was that James had a big bicep and a double barrel like chest, he was a body builder, his father on the other hand was attractively slim "My son don't you know that such girl is not good for you"? His father opened the discussion on Janet, instantly James became sad "But what is wrong with Janet" isn't she beautiful enough to be my girl friend"? he was looking deep into his father's eyes as he inquired from his father, "Beautiful yes, but my son if you want girls that are even more beautiful than Janet and from rich homes too, I can introduce some of them to you to choose from" his father responded, " No dad, you can't introduce anybody to me, I have the right to choose for myself" James chipped in "you are quite right there my son, but if you want to choose, choose from the right source, not somebody from the slum, O come on James give me a break, where is your thinking cap'? his father added and asked a question too," 'Dad, it is Janet, I want to be my girl friend" " James was standing looking annoyed, "Then you must be joking; James you are Joking, I mean how can you stand here and tell me you want to go out with a nobody, have you forgotten my status in the society? His father retorted angrily, anger was in the air, James angrily walked away, "James come back here, I say come back here" his father was barking at him like a soldier barking out instruction to a junior officer, but James did not listen to him.

Chapter 5

That night James was angry all through because of his parents stance concerning Janet, he thought about the matter seriously and concluded that he was going to leave the house. That same night at about 11pm, he got into his car and left the house in a state of annoyance. The gate man tried to stop him to no avail. "Oga James where you dey go this night? The gateman Inquired, in Pidgin English, but James who was always friendly with all his father's domestic workers did not respond, but quickly drove off immediately the gateman opened the gate, after he forcefully made the gateman to open the gate.

Chapter 6

The following day after he left their house, James went to Janet's place of abode. He drove his Prado Jeep to the slum, and it was the cynosure of all eyes, as he parked the car, two boys with chubby faces walked up to the car happily, James inquired from them about Janet's place, and they directed him. As he was about knocking at the door, the house was a typical house for the low class citizen, it was the face me I face you type of house. It was as if Janet knew he was going to come, she got money from her boy friend who was so much in love with her and her parents loved the young man, but somehow Janet just could not love him in equal measure; she felt that she did not have a future with him even though he had a steady off and on job and very good looking with good height too. She had a new hair and nice work on her eyelash and finger nails too, these made her attractive the more, as she opened the door after James knocked, he felt like grabbing her very firmly in his big arms, but looking at her face, his mind changed completely, she was frowning " James who are you looking for here"? "Janet I came to apologize to you, I understand how you feel, after my parents behaved rudely to you" James sounded very sober and thoughtful, "James you don't have to apologize, they are your parents, if they feel I am not good enough for you, I don't think there is anything you can do about that" her face was firm and still frowned, James held her passionately, " Janet that is not true; fine they are my parents, but they can't decide for me who to go out with" James uttered "So James what do you intend to do now that your parents don't want me"? she looked deep into his eyes as she inquired, "I believe if we prove to them we are deeply in love, they will have no option than to support us", James affirmed, "Honestly, I think that will be difficult to achieve, I am sorry to say that your parents are arrogant" Janet uttered face still frowned "I know, but if we stick to our love they will have a change of attitude towards you" James continued, "James your parents don't want you to go out with some one like me so leave it that way", her defense was still stout "Janet, I can't leave it that way and for your information I have moved out of the house" James still pressed to achieve his aim "why? It is not necessary" Janet surprised uttered, "it is necessary, I am presently staying with a friend" "James added.

Chapter 7

James's father had an elder sister, her name was aunty Dayo. She was born in Lagos while James's father was born in their place of origin Delta State. She was a stunning beauty, and attractively slim with a disarming smile, her smile could melt the hardest of hearts, strange enough as a lady she was taller than James and his father at 6feet 7inches tall; before finally settling down in marriage, she had a problem finding her dream man; she wanted somebody taller than she was, but ended up marrying a man 5inches less in height. Her husband, who was a senior naval officer, was a 6feet two inches giant and very beefy.

She visited her younger brother after been there for some time she asked "I am just wondering, where is James?. I have been in this house for 10minutes, and have not seen him around, that is unusual" she confirmed and questioned her younger brother "you won't believe it, for the past 3days we have been looking for him" James father said "where has he gone to, didn't he tell anybody"? Aunty looking shocked inquired, "he did not mention anything to anybody about his where about" James father revealed, "Did he quarrel with anybody"? Aunty further probed, "Actually, he brought one girl from a poor home and said he wanted to fall in love with her, but we advised him against such action, considering her poor status" James father reacted "absolute rubbish; why would you and your wife dissuade a young man from following his heart desire"? She asked very angrily," But aunty the girl is from a poor home, James cannot go out with just a low status girl" he confirmed, "Charles how come you have forgotten so soon, that when you married James's mother, she was from a poor home, you helped her to become who she is today, now she wants to send away a girl from a poor home away, that is absolute rubbish" aunty Dayo was still angry.

Chapter 8

Aunty Dayo was about entering a supermarket after coming out from her car standing taller than all other customers coming and going out of the supermarket, she decided to call James first "James........ I have been trying to get you on line............why have you refused to pick your parents

106

call……………..Okay James my darling I understand your part…………..Okay don't worry I have trashed out the issue with them, so you can return home" she hanged up chuckling as she walked into the exquisite supermarket; James and aunty Dayo had strong link, they were like mother and son incidentally, she only had 3 girls, so she saw James as her only male child, and they look so much alike, it was just that James had a massive body frame, but they had a very similar facial looks.

Chapter 9

Aunty Dayo had finally settled the problem between James, Janet and his parents; they were all sitting inside James father's exquisite and beautiful sitting room. "Janet, I want to personally apologize to you for all the heartaches I have caused you; I must confess, I was the one who encouraged my husband not to welcome you" James mother was surprisingly apologetic to Janet "Thank you ma for accepting me" Janet reacted very shyly "personally, I will apologize to both of you James and Janet I am very sorry" his father did the right thing apologizing to both of them. He later gave Janet a job, and financed their elaborate wedding.

NOTES:

If I am to write this story, in full I will introduce many dimensions using characters and situations to further entertain, in form and educate my readers.

Did you notice how I use the situation of a rainy day and national stadium in chapter one, as well as other chapters that I used other situations? Did you notice the support characters: James's parents and aunty Dayo? Did you notice the lead characters James and Janet? Did you notice the minor characters, the young boys with chubby faces?

HOW TO EASILY MAKE IT AS A NOVELIST:

First and foremost you have to be a member of the Association of Nigeria Authors (ANA), you can make inquiry of ANA at the national theater Iganmu Lagos I strongly believe that they have branches Nation Wide. However if you are outside Nigeria, you can find association of writers in your territory and start mingling with them.   After you complete writing your novel ensure you get it registered with the copy right commission, and get your International serial book number (ISBN) from national library to reduce piracy on your work. You can start small by typing your novel and there after make neat and clear copies of them and serial bind them and then send to your family members, bosses, and friends (they must be people you are sure can assist you) asking them to support you with finance to enable you kick start your career. Marketing is the biggest problem of novelists, however if you have a good novel you can approach one of the publishers and marketing firms around to publish and market your work for you; you can reach a percentage ratio of how to share the profit with the firm, however I strongly suggest that you should be on the "low side" for your first work, if it does well in the market, you can there after request for a bigger percentage from your subsequent works. Always get somebody (an expert) to edit for you. YOU CAN ALSO SELL YOUR NOVEL VIA THE INTERNET VISIT(amazon is your best bet, there other platforms that can help you to sell your novels, you can check them out in the net) . You can write 2novels per year. DO YOU WANT ME TO GHOST WRITE FOR YOU? I.E. I DEVELOP YOUR STORY OR IDEA INTO A NOVEL, AND YOU TAKE THE CREDIT FOR IT, (WHILE YOU PAY ME MY FEE ONLY)? Reach out to me. (after sometime you can as well be a ghost writer for others too, and they will pay you cool cash)

EPILOGUE

This manual vital ingredients in the arts of creative story writing, creative screenplay writing, rudiments of film production, some jobs in Nollywood to do and as well as in the creative/entertainment industry on full time or part time basis, plus many unseen business angles is written for both young and old persons that have strong desire to succeed in these arts.

Are you a graduate or undergraduate of any discipline, old and young school leaver, employed, under employed, unemployed, retired but not tired? And have an "unstoppable force and unquenchable thirst" for these arts , then this manual is for you, with this information manual, you can easily attain lofty heights in these arts. This manual is aimed at awakening the giant in you.

These arts need consistency, commitment, passion, "thinking outside the box" they are vital tools that are necessary and will ensure you succeed in these arts; this manual is targeted at ensuring that these are easily attained by intending practitioners.

One special feature of the Nollywood/creative and entertainment industry is that it can engage enough persons as possible on part time or full time basis, especially for those that have real passion for the industry. The industry provides various jobs on full time or part time basis that can be combined by interested and deeply passionate individuals to make ends meet, considering the lack of jobs in our society,

Nollywood/creative entertainment industry serve as succour to deeply interested individuals. The manual also expose many unseen business angles in these arts that can be explored by individuals to impact positively to the growth of the economy as well as contributing to a better society, by applying them in any chosen area of the industry.

Welcome to the industry that welcomes everybody irrespective of age, gender, religious believe, height or size. The only industry that does not discriminate. Educational background is not a barrier in this ever bubbling industry, so far you can speak, read and write and can always put on your " thinking cap rightly", you are welcome.

LUCKY ODILI

(STORY DEVELOPER, STORYTELLER, SCREENWRITER, NOVELIST, DRAMATIST, SONGWRITER, DANCE CONCEPT DEVELOPER, FILM PRODUCER, CREATIVE ENTREPRENEUR, ARTISTIC FILM DIRECTOR, HUMAN CAPITAL DEVELOPER, PUBLIC AFFAIRS ANALYST)

08135106497, 07059603163